Breaking Chains, Building Dreams: From Incarceration To Inspiration

K. Rachaan Smit
Copyright © 202

All rights reserved.

ISBN: 979-8-9866328-1-0

DEDICATION

To my incredible wife, Jinelys, whose love and unwavering support have been my guiding light through every challenge. To my Aunty Valencia whose encouragement lifted me during my darkest moments, Aunt Paula and Brenda for being invested in my childhood with nurturing and love. Unc (Tommy) for his wisdom and simplicity, and Cousin Talaya for giving me my flowers while I'm still here. To my friend Amyr for standing by me with loyalty. To my mother, Jacqueline, and my father, Alphonso, for the gift of life and the values you instilled in me. To my big brother, Mike, for your inspiration and guidance. And to my six beautiful children—Paris, Queen, Jihad, Haiti, Kanela, and Enaji—thank you for giving me a reason to strive for greatness. This journey is for you all.

TABLE OF CONTENTS

	Introduction	Pg.1
C1	Roots of Resilience	Pg.4
C2	The Wrong Associations	Pg.6
C3	Shattered Dreams	Pg.16
C4	Road to Redemption	Pg.21
C5	Rebuilding a Life	Pg.25
C6	Family and Relationships	Pg.28
C7	Success and It's Discontents	Pg.32
C8	Giving Back and Advocating For Change	Pg.37
	Conclusion: A Message of Hope	Pg.45
	Note to the Reader	Pg.47
	Organizations	Pg.49
	Books	Pg.50
	About the Author	Pg.51

ACKNOWLEDGMENTS

I would like to extend my heartfelt gratitude to everyone who has supported me on this journey, whether directly or indirectly. Your encouragement, love, and belief in my potential have made this book possible.

Thank you all for being a part of my story.

INTRODUCTION

In a world quick to judge and slow to understand, the narrative surrounding those who find themselves behind bars is often one of guilt and shame. Yet, my story—and the stories of countless others challenges this perception. I drafted this book not just to share my journey, but to shed light on a harsh reality: not everyone in prison is guilty of a crime. Many, particularly young Black men, face systemic barriers that lead to wrongful convictions and a lack of support from the very communities that should uplift them.

The court system is broken, and it doesn't always get it right. I want to remind my children that they come from an honorable father and to show my community that I am worthy of respect. I subscribe to the idea that ex-convicts are deserving of a clean slate once debt to society is paid and full, and this claim is underscored by the fact that the 47th president, Donald Trump, now holds office with 34 felony convictions. This reality highlights a stark privilege afforded to certain sectors of society, standing in sharp contrast to the experiences of young Black males from humble beginnings, who often face a lifetime of stigma and barriers long after serving their time. It is crucial to recognize that the person behind the bars is not defined solely by their past mistakes.

Growing up, I was filled with dreams and aspirations, particularly my passion for Hip Hop. I have always been a writer at heart, using words to touch people and convey the struggles and triumphs of life. My dream was to become a Hip-Hop artist, to share my voice and experiences with the world. I want to advocate for youth who are misunderstood and misrepresented, those who come from backgrounds similar to mine and face the same challenges.

The absence of a supportive network can be devastating. In my experience, friends and family often abandon those accused of crimes, fearing judgment or embarrassment. This abandonment can leave individuals feeling isolated and hopeless, especially when they need support the most. I want to emphasize that it is crucial to stand by those who are struggling, for the child who cries out for attention through their actions may be a future leader waiting to be nurtured.

As I reflect on my own journey, I recognize the importance of self- worth and self-esteem. Though I am naturally introverted around strangers, I have learned to embrace my identity with confidence. I want to reintroduce myself to the world—not as a product of my past, but as a person who has overcome adversity and emerged stronger. My mission is to remind others that we must not let potential leaders slip through the cracks of life. We never know when the overlooked child, yearning for support, will rise to greatness if only given the chance.

This book is a testament to resilience, hope, and the unwavering belief that it is never too late to change the narrative. I continue to fight for justice and understanding, not just for myself, but for all those who share similar backgrounds and experiences. As long as I am in this world, I plan to be a force to be reckoned with—a beacon of motivation for those who feel lost and forgotten. Join me on this journey as we explore the complexities of prison reform, the power of community support, and the indomitable spirit of those who refuse to be defined by their past. Together, we can challenge perceptions, foster understanding, and create a world where everyone has the opportunity to thrive.

CHAPTER 1: ROOTS OF RESILIENCE

I was raised by my mother in a single-parent household, alongside my older brother, who is four and a half years my senior. My mother was a fun-spirited woman, known for her ability to host family gatherings and parties. She was the quintessential "girl's girl," with a love for travel and a heart full of warmth. Our modest Baptist roots meant that my early childhood years were marked by infrequent trips to church, but the values instilled in me by my mother were profound nonetheless.

My brother was a popular kid in the neighborhood, ambitious and mature beyond his years. He took on a sense of responsibility that came from helping my mother provide in the absence of a father. He was my role model, and I looked up to him in many ways. For as long as I can remember, I harbored aspirations of becoming a Hip-Hop artist and ladies' man, even as a child. I was captivated by the images of rappers and street hustlers, drawn to their finest fashions and the possessions that defined success.

To me, these figures were heroes. They embodied what success looked like through the eyes of a kid sitting on the stairways, dreaming of BMX bikes and everything else that defined my generation—like getting my first pair of suede Pumas, a boom box, and rocking a fresh high-top fade. The allure of that lifestyle was intoxicating, and it fueled my ambitions. The only people around me who had money were those who sold drugs, and they were not much older than I was. This environment shaped my aspirations, even though my true passions lay in Hip-Hop and the pursuit of cute girls.

My traditional values were rooted in the teachings of the church and the lessons imparted by my mother. Yet, my ambition, style, and love for breakdancing were heavily influenced by my brother, who also fell victim to the criminal justice system. His experiences served as both a cautionary tale and a source of inspiration for me. I admired his resilience, but I also saw the harsh realities of a system that often failed young men like him.

As I navigated my childhood, my dreams crystallized: I wanted to become a wealthy Hip Hop star, someone who could rise above the circumstances that surrounded me. I envisioned a life filled with success, respect, and the ability to provide for my family in ways that my mother had always dreamed of. Little did I know that the journey ahead would be fraught with challenges that would test my resilience and redefine my understanding of success.

CHAPTER 2: THE WRONG ASSOCIATIONS

My good intentions often led to poor choices, rooted in my belief that everyone deserves a chance. I opened myself up to others, extending my loyalty and respect, only to find that many around me lacked the same values that I held dear. This disparity would soon become a defining aspect of my personal brand, shaping my relationships and experiences in ways I could never have anticipated.

After we moved from my childhood neighborhood, my mother sought to provide a better environment for us, one that would shield us from the negative effects of the crack epidemic that was beginning to take hold of our community. The allure of quick money from drug dealing had captivated my older brother, complementing his ambitions but also pulling him deeper into a world fraught with danger. In this new neighborhood, I found myself surrounded by kids born to stable homes who craved the credibility that came from being associated with the hood, a lifestyle glorified by media culture. They romanticized the struggles without understanding the harsh realities that accompanied them, while all I wanted was a life of stability.

Despite their better circumstances, many of these kids were envious of the freedom and exposure I had. They looked at me with a mix of admiration and resentment, threatened by my rising popularity with the girls as I began to mature. I was the kid with the least resources, yet I somehow attracted attention in a predominant military and middle-class area. My naivety regarding social etiquette and the pretentious behavior of my peers made me an outsider, but it also made me intriguing.

As I navigated this environment, I found myself drawn to the thrill of early experiences—having sex and gaining access to drugs— without much interest in the consequences that came with them. I was caught in a whirlwind of adolescent exploration, unaware of how these associations would shape my future. The allure of fitting in and being accepted often clouded my judgment, leading me to align myself with individuals who did not share my values or aspirations.

By the time I became a sophomore in high school, I had quite the following as I began to hone my rap skills, all while becoming very promiscuous and popular with the young ladies. I convinced myself that I had friends who wanted to see me shine, but more than a few were only around to block my shine or steal it for themselves, feeling that they were more worthy of having what I had established for myself. I allowed the influence of my drug-dealing big homies, with all their style and charisma, to shape how I presented myself. Most kids during that time had been misled to believe that having a stake in street culture was a rite of passage. Since I had a front row seat to the game, and was legitimately cut from the cloth of the guys they so desperately imitated, I began to find myself unguarded among an army of posing friends who wanted to ride my wave.

The further I got away from my childhood friends, the cloudier my judgment became. Even though my childhood neighborhood was challenging, we had real love around us, and, we had the same things, so everyone felt like family. The occasional riffs that arose from the frustrations of living in poverty and the effects of coming from a broken home were nothing compared to the sense of community we shared. In contrast, my unfamiliar environment was filled with superficial connections, where loyalty was often conditional, and friendships were transactional.

As I reflect on this period, I realize that my journey was not just about the choices I made, but also about the people I chose to surround myself with. The wrong associations can lead to a path of destruction, and I was about to learn that lesson the hard way. My good intentions, coupled with a desire for acceptance, would soon lead me down a road I never intended to travel—one that would challenge my resilience and test my resolve, culminating in my incarceration.

With all the distractions and pitfalls that come with self-discovery as a teenager, I still managed to graduate from high school. As a graduation gift, my mom got me a round-trip ticket to Connecticut to spend a week with a friend who had come down to visit during my graduation week. This friend was also a member of my first rap group, and we had plans to do some recording, hoping to make something of my music before I felt the pressure of having to choose between college or the military—

both of which were expected paths for most kids of Generation X upon completing high school.

It was important to me to show my mom that her efforts in raising my brother and me alone did not go unnoticed. Despite my mannish ways often drawing unwarranted attention, I wanted her to know that her son would eventually become someone great, despite the odds stacked against us. I was determined to make something of my music career within a year of graduating; otherwise, I would be heading to college, even against my will. The military was not an option for me, and I wanted to ensure that those who may have counted my immediate family out for lacking structure would witness my resilience to rise above my obstacles. I wanted to give both my mom and my brother a sense of purpose and pride.

Once I returned from my graduation trip, armed with a hot song I could not wait to shop around, I decided to fly out to New York to spend time with another friend and promote my music. It was during this trip that I realized the magnitude of the world I was stepping into. The energy of the city was intoxicating, and I felt a sense of possibility that I had never experienced before. I was surrounded by aspiring artists, producers, and dreamers, all chasing their own versions of success.

However, the allure of the city also came with its own set of distractions. The same charisma that drew me to the music scene also opened doors to the wrong associations. I found myself mingling with individuals who were more interested in the lifestyle than the craft. The pressure to fit in and be accepted was palpable, and I began to lose sight of my original intentions. The excitement of being in

New York, coupled with the thrill of newfound attention, clouded my judgment.

As I navigated this vibrant yet chaotic environment, I felt the weight of my aspirations pressing down on me. I was determined to make a name for myself, but the distractions were relentless. I had to remind myself of the promise I made to my mother and the vision I had for my future. I wanted to be a beacon of hope for my family, proving that we could rise above our circumstances.

Yet, as I immersed myself in this world, I began to realize that the very associations I had sought out for support were leading me down a path that could jeopardize everything I had worked for. The allure of street credibility and the desire to be seen as part of the culture I admired began to overshadow my true passion for music. I was at a crossroads, and the choices I made in the coming weeks would have lasting consequences.

Having access to New York, where I would often spend summers on Long Island as a kid, made my dream of becoming a Hip-Hop artist feel attainable. The summer following my graduation was different, though. I was not being received by my grandmother and father; instead, I was traveling on my own accord in pursuit of my dreams. I made it my duty to frequent the city as often as it would take to accomplish what I had set out to do.

As I began to move forward, I noticed that my peers were developing greater desires that their parents were not willing to finance. Everyone started taking chances in the name of getting money so they too, could experience the world at their discretion and without the consent of their parents.

It was a reckless time, fueled by ambition and the desire for independence.

One day, a friend who was down on his luck approached me with a stolen check he had received from a robbery. Caught up in the momentum of my own aspirations and the excitement of the city, I made a fateful decision. I took him to the bank to cash the check, completely unaware of its origins. I was blinded by the thrill of the moment, thinking I was helping a friend in need.

Needless to say, a few days later, my photo was being flashed on the news as a suspect in an armed robbery. It was during the airing of "Martin," a show that was at the peak of its ratings, so everyone and their mother saw it. The fallout was immediate and devastating. All the people I thought were my friends began making reports and writing statements about who I was and where I lived. They had had enough of me parading around like a big deal, despite my humble demeanor.

The irony of it all was that just as I was coming of age and life seemed to be aligning with the stars, the very people I had surrounded myself with were eager to see me fall. My rising popularity had made me a target, and the jealousy that brewed beneath the surface erupted when I found myself in trouble. The betrayal cut deep, and I was left to grapple with the consequences of my choices.

In that moment, I realized how quickly the tides could turn. The same ambition that had driven me to chase my dreams now felt like a double-edged sword. I had been so focused on the pursuit of success that I had neglected to recognize the dangers lurking in the shadows. The wrong associations had led me down a path I never intended to travel, and now I was facing the harsh reality of my actions.

As I sat in the aftermath of this chaos, I understood that my journey was not just about the music or the fame; it was about the choices I made and the people I chose to trust. The allure of street credibility and the desire to fit in had clouded my judgment, and I was about to learn a lesson that would change the course of my life forever.

The emotional and psychological impact of being imprisoned for a crime you did not commit is a heavy burden to bear. It makes you feel helpless, causes you to question God, and leaves you grappling with feelings of unworthiness and inferiority. In those dark moments, you come to understand just how broken the system is. Some people believe you are guilty simply because you have been convicted, and that stigma can be suffocating.

During my trial, I had a prominent lawyer in my town, Peter Johnson, take the stand as a sworn witness on my behalf. On the day and time the armed robbery took place— the very crime I was arrested for—I was in court with Mr. Johnson on unrelated charges. Even with a proven alibi and a typed transcript from a court stenographer to support our claims, I was railroaded and sentenced to 20 years with the possibility of parole after 10. The victims were coerced into identifying me as the perpetrator, claiming they were sure it was me because I allegedly robbed them without a mask.

I could not believe the system was that corrupt, willing to take my life away despite the evidence that proved my innocence. Even with a lawyer's testimony, no one believed I was innocent—except for my grandmother. She was my rock, the only person who fought tirelessly to free me. Her unwavering belief in my innocence was a beacon of hope in an otherwise bleak situation.

I was mischievous, yes, and I came from a neighborhood plagued by drugs and crime, but I was no robber. I had dreams of becoming a Hip-hop artist, and I wanted to make something of myself. Yet, as I sat in that cold, unforgiving cell, I realized that my aspirations were slipping further away. The weight of my circumstances pressed down on me, but I was determined not to let it crush my spirit.

While I was out on bond, life took another unexpected turn—I became a father. The news filled me with a mix of joy and fear. I knew I had to make a choice: I could either continue down the path of music and risk everything, or I could take the responsible route and pursue an education. I decided to go to college, hoping to create a better future for my child and myself.

The decision was not easy. I felt torn between my passion for rap and the responsibilities of fatherhood. But I knew that I had to rise above my circumstances, not just for me, but for my child. I wanted to break the cycle of hardship that had plagued my family for generations. I wanted to show my son that despite the odds, it was possible to overcome adversity and build a life filled with purpose.

As I embarked on this new journey, I carried the weight of my past with me. The wrong associations had led me to a place I never wanted to be, but I was determined to learn from my mistakes. I would not let my experiences define me; instead, I would use them as fuel to propel me forward. The road ahead would be challenging, but I was ready to fight for my future and the future of my child.

My life had been stolen. I was never even given the opportunity to tell my side of the story. Despite having a solid alibi and a strong belief in my innocence, I had no intention of cooperating with a system that had already made up its mind about me. My upbringing taught me to mind my own business and to see as little as possible when it came to other people's affairs. I had always believed that staying out of trouble meant staying out of others' business, but in this case, it only left me vulnerable.

I went to prison nevertheless, and that day, my dreams shattered. The walls that surrounded me felt like a prison not just of steel and concrete, but of despair and hopelessness. I was thrust into a world that was foreign to me, a place where my aspirations were reduced to mere memories. The vibrant dreams of becoming a Hip-Hop artist, of making music that resonated with others, were replaced by the stark reality of confinement.

As I sat in my cell, I could not help but reflect on the choices that had led me here. The wrong associations, the misguided trust in people who did not have my best interests at heart, and the reckless decisions I had made all culminated in this moment. I felt a profound sense of loss—not just for the life I had envisioned, but for the relationships I had taken for granted and the opportunities that had slipped through my fingers.

Prison was a harsh teacher, and I was forced to confront the consequences of my actions. I had to grapple with the reality that my future was now uncertain, and the dreams I had nurtured for so long felt like distant echoes. The weight of my circumstances pressed down on me, but I knew I had to find a way to rise above it all. In despair, I began to search for a glimmer of hope. I realized that while my physical freedom had been taken from me, my spirit remained unbroken. I had to find a way to channel my pain into something productive. I started writing—lyrics, poems, reflections on my experiences. It became my lifeline, a way to express the turmoil within me and to keep my dreams alive, even in the darkest of places. Though my dreams had been shattered, I refused to let them die. I began to understand that resilience is born from adversity, and I was determined to emerge from this experience stronger than before. I would not allow the wrong associations to define my future. Instead, I would use this time to reflect, grow, and prepare for the day when I would reclaim my life and my dreams.

CHAPTER 3: SHATTERED DREAMS

Just when I was beginning to feel like an adult, having spent year out of the shadows of my big homies and riding my wave into a promising future, everything came crashing down. I lost all momentum and suddenly found myself engulfed in a deep depression. My brother had been incarcerated himself for two years, serving a 25-year sentence, and for the second time in prison, I felt the weight of the world on my shoulders. I tried to fill his shoes and become the man of the house, but I failed. This left one of my nephews to be raised alone by my mother, alongside my two children, who were born just 13 months apart. To add to the chaos, I would later learn that I had another child on the way shortly after I was locked up.

Everything I had worked for, everything I had built, seemed to vanish in the blink of an eye. The dreams I had nurtured, the aspirations I had chased, were now distant memories. The only things I retained were my determination, my integrity, and my ability to effectively communicate my thoughts and feelings through my pen. Writing became my refuge, a way to process the whirlwind of emotions that threatened to consume me.

In the depths of my despair, I began to realize that I was not alone. Countless others had been railroaded in a similar fashion, their dreams and aspirations snatched away by an unforgiving system that swallowed Black youth whole and spat them out once there was no more life left in them. I found solace in the company of likeminded individuals who shared my struggles. Together, we built a community within those prison walls, exchanging information, ideas, and books that would serve us well in the future.

No matter how hard the days became, we knew we had to push through. We convinced one another that there was still a lot of life left ahead of us, and that we needed to be prepared to take on the challenges of our future. We shared our stories, our hopes, and our fears, and in doing so, we forged bonds that transcended our circumstances.

Through our conversations, I learned that resilience was not just about enduring hardship; it was about finding strength in vulnerability and using our experiences to fuel our ambitions. We discussed our dreams of freedom, of making something of ourselves once we were released, and of breaking the cycles that had held us captive for too long.

As I poured my heart into my writing, I began to see a glimmer of hope. I realized that while my dreams had been shattered, they were not beyond repair. I could still rebuild, still strive for a future that was worth fighting for. The journey ahead would be long and fraught with challenges, but I was determined to rise from the ashes of my past and reclaim my life. In that prison cell, I found a renewed sense of purpose. I would not let my circumstances define me. Instead, I would use my experiences to inspire others, to advocate for change, and to show that even in the darkest of times, there is always a path to redemption.

After five years of exhausting appeals and motions for a new trial, surrendered my fight. I adjusted my focus more on my return to reality and much less on getting out early. The relentless pursuit of justice had drained me, and I realized that I needed to redirect my energy toward preparing for life beyond the prison walls. Reading and working out became my therapy, alongside creative writing. These activities provided an escape, a way to maintain my sanity in an environment designed to break spirits.

    The turning point for me came when I began to get serious about barbering as a potential career path. I had a few years of shade tree experience, and it felt relatable to Hip Hop in the sense that most of the styles I was cutting were heavily influenced by the looks that many rising artists sported. Haircuts do wonders for a prisoner's self-esteem, and if done well enough, you could earn your keep cutting hair—especially on visitation days when family and friends came to see their loved ones.

    I quickly became an asset on every prison yard I graced. I was good with a razor and a comb, able to cut hair as well as any barber could with a set of clippers and trimmers. I knew that if I could earn my way in prison by cutting hair, it would be simple once I returned home. My mother had invested in a pair of clippers for my brother and me when we were younger, teaching us how to cut our own hair. This not only saved us money but also instilled a sense of pride in our appearance.

Cutting hair in prison gave me a greater sense of purpose. It allowed me to connect with others, to share stories, and to create a sense of community among the men who sat in my chair. Each haircut was an opportunity to uplift someone's spirits, to help them feel a little more human in a place that often stripped away one's identity. I found joy in transforming someone's look, and in turn, it transformed my own outlook on life.

Moreover, my skills helped me leverage relationships with the prison guards, who also desired my hair-cutting services. I became known for my talent, and it opened doors that I never expected. The guards would often request haircuts, and in exchange, I gained a bit of respect and leniency. It was a delicate balance, but I navigated it with care, understanding that my ability to cut hair was an asset in a place where power dynamics were constantly shifting.

As I honed my barbering skills, I began to envision a future where I could turn this passion into a legitimate career. I started to dream again—not just of freedom, but of a life where I could use my talents to support my family and build a better future. The more I focused on my craft, the more I realized that I could create a path for myself, one that was rooted in hard work and determination.

In those moments of transformation, I found a renewed sense of hope. I was no longer just a prisoner; I was an artist, a creator, and a man with a purpose. The dreams I thought were shattered began to take shape again, and I was determined to rise from the ashes of my past, ready to embrace the challenges that lay ahead.

CHAPTER 4: ROAD TO REDEMPTION

The steps I took to prepare for reintegration into society consisted of a lot of reading, researching, and studying various subjects (religion, relationships, business, psychology, politics, and strategy). I immersed myself in the teachings of influential thinkers, with Robert Greene's *The 48 Laws of Power* and *The Art of Seduction*, as well as Sun Tzu's *The Art of War*, among my favorite studies. I had always been intrigued by the ways in which people could persuade and manipulate situations to work in their favor, exercising mental capacity over physical strength.

One of the most significant inspirations during my time in prison was the record of Malcolm X. His hard work and dedication to his studies while incarcerated resulted in him becoming a great leader and teacher of truth in the Black community. His journey reminded me that self-education could be a powerful tool for transformation, and I was determined to follow in his footsteps.

I poured over the words of Maya Angelou, James Baldwin, George Jackson, Anthony Browder, and Ralph Ellison, drawn to their intellectual quality that helped raise my consciousness and broaden my perspective. I also enjoyed reading novels, particularly those by Robert Beck (Iceberg Slim) and Donald Goines. Their street references and the characters they created resonated with my own experiences, and I found a strong curiosity about gangster and pimp culture that mirrored the realities of my life. This fascination should not surprise anyone, given how young Black men are often introduced to ideas about their rise into manhood in neighborhoods where male role models are absent.

To calm my busy mind filled with thoughts of returning home and what awaited me, I began to meditate to the sounds of jazz and orchestrated music before bed. The soothing melodies helped me find peace amidst the chaos of my thoughts. Sade's voice often serenaded me when I needed a female presence to soothe my longing for companionship, while Bob Marley's Legend album provided a soundtrack of hope and resilience. His messages of love and perseverance resonated deeply with me, reminding me that there was a world beyond the prison walls waiting for me.

During this time, I also participated in several programs that helped me grow. The barbering program allowed me to hone my skills while providing a sense of purpose. I joined a Creating Value Systems group, which focused on personal development and accountability. Additionally, I attended both Muslim and Christian services to keep my spirit uplifted and to support the brothers I met who were involved in prison ministry in several ways.

Over the years of my incarceration, I grew remarkably close to my paternal aunt, Valencia. She assured me that I was capable and made me accountable for being in my predicament, whether guilty or not. She helped me understand how my choices, along with my circumstances, had led me to this point. Though she would be supportive, she insisted that she would not be supporting a victim but a capable young man. My aunt Valencia reminded me that I was intelligent enough to take responsibility for my own life, and I could not thank her enough for her tough love, consistent communication, and understanding.

There was also a childhood friend of mine who was a writer herself. She somehow found me, and we began to write each other often, visiting me quite frequently despite the challenges of distance and circumstance. Her unwavering support meant the world to me, and we grew remarkably close. She encouraged me to write more, sent me writing exercises, and eventually helped me get one of my works published. This experience was transformative, reinforcing my belief in the power of words and the importance of sharing my story.

As I delved into these studies and embraced the power of music, I began to envision a future where I could apply the knowledge I had gained. I wanted to be more than just a product of my environment; I wanted to be a force for change. I realized that my experiences, both good and bad, had equipped me with unique insights that could help others navigate their own struggles.

I started to formulate a plan for my reintegration. I would seek out mentors who could guide me in my pursuit of a career in barbering and beyond. I wanted to build a network of support that would help me stay grounded and focused on my goals. I knew that the road ahead would be challenging, but I was determined to face it head-on.

The more I prepared, the more I felt a sense of empowerment. I was no longer just a prisoner; I was a student of life, ready to embrace the opportunities that awaited me. I understood that redemption was not just about reclaiming my freedom; it was about transforming my life and using my experiences to uplift others.

As I approached the end of my sentence, I felt a renewed sense of purpose. I was ready to step into the world with confidence, armed with the knowledge and skills, I had acquired during my time in prison. The road to redemption was not easy, but I was committed to walking it with integrity and determination, ready to make a positive impact on my life and the lives of those around me.

CHAPTER 5: REBUILDING A LIFE

After a long 10 years of confinement, I looked forward to nothing more than reuniting with my loved ones. My brother, who had been released six months prior, along with my nephew, came to pick me up. I had been restless for months leading up to the day of my release. It felt like a dream come true. I was elated to see my family, but as soon as we started to ride home, I was consumed with thoughts of being free. Everything we talked about felt vague because I just could not get out of my head. My day had come, I was finally free!

The weather was perfect for August, and I can remember taking in my hometown for the first time in what seemed like ages. I was trying to see how much had changed in the landscape and how much I could remember. I was ready for anything and everything, and the anticipation of going to the studio left me hopeful. However, my main goals at the time were to enroll in college, find gainful employment, and reacquaint myself with my family, particularly my children.

Shortly after my release, two of my children came to live with me at my mother's house. It was a bittersweet reunion, filled with joy and the weight of responsibility. I wanted to be the father they deserved, to make up for lost time and create new memories together. I found a barbershop to work out of just a few miles away, and I worked full-time at the barbershop during the day while attending barber school in the evenings.

As I settled into my new routine, I noticed how much the social tone of society had shifted during my time away. Technology had advanced, and cultural trends had evolved. But if I had survived gladiator school—meaning prison—this would be a piece of cake. My tunnel vision helped me navigate distractions with discipline. I had a plan to execute, and I understood that setting goals was important because it gave me something to work toward. The more I accomplished, the more I realized how much I was validating myself.

During my time in college training, I worked for two different barbershops, first to get my barber license and then to obtain my instructor training license. Shortly after I ended my tenure at the college, I applied for my barbershop license and went on to open my own barbershop. All my hard work was paying off; I just made it look easy because I was well-prepared to carry the burden of entrepreneurship.

Through this journey, I learned to remain humble and to be a student of life. I learned patience and the importance of perseverance. I discovered that a person's value is measured not by what they can acquire or possess, but by what they can live without. I didn't forget that things could be removed from your life in the blink of an eye, and I made it a point to take nothing for granted.

As I built my business and reconnected with my family, I felt a sense of fulfillment that I had longed for during my years of confinement. I was no longer just a man who had been in prison; I was a father, a business owner, and a member of my community. I was determined to make a positive impact, not just for myself, but for my children and those around me.

Rebuilding my life was a continuous process, filled with challenges and triumphs. Each day brought new lessons, and I embraced them all. I was ready to face whatever came next, armed with the knowledge that I had the power to shape my own destiny.

CHAPTER 6: FAMILY AND RELATIONSHIPS

What I began to understand is that relationships with family and friends were strained due to the amount of time I spent in prison and the distance it created between us. I did not know them as they had become, and surely, they did not know me. More often than I was comfortable with, they acted as if they did, claiming to be in tune with the person I had become and witnessing my growth into manhood. I am certain they could not grasp the concept of my evolution. In engaging their curiosities about the man before them, I often led them away from getting to know me anew, allowing them to fancy their own imaginations about the man they thought I should be.

Family members who were not supportive felt justified in believing I was in denial about my transgressions rather than accepting the fact that they simply lacked the courage to stand up against this whitewashed system of oppression. They failed to defend the innocence of a young Black male who came from a place where kids could be typecast and exposed to things even adults should not have to witness. The weight of their judgment felt heavy, and I often found myself grappling with the reality that some of my own family members could not see beyond the label of "ex-convict."

Given my popularity growing up, many of my peers silently gloated in the fact that I had been humbled. In many ways, they felt they had surpassed me in experiences and achievements. They figured they had all matured while I had not, and since I was a measuring stick for them, they were pleased with themselves. What malice and resentment they must have harbored, believing that my struggles somehow validated their own choices.

Reconnecting with family and friends was a delicate process. I wanted to share my journey, to show them the man I had become, but I often felt like I was speaking a different language. The experiences I had endured in prison had changed me, and I was no longer the same person they remembered. I had grown in ways that were difficult for them to understand, and I often felt like an outsider in my own family.

Despite these challenges, I was determined to rebuild those relationships. I wanted to show my family that I was committed to being a better person, a better father, and a better son. I reached out to those who were willing to engage with me, sharing my story and my aspirations. I wanted them to see that I was not defined by my past but by my determination to create a brighter future.

Rebuilding trust was exceedingly difficult for me after I learned that I had been betrayed a million times over by people I had been loyal to, those to whom I had given the benefit of the doubt. People I had not known as well as I thought I did, would soon reveal they never truly knew me at all. The obsession with girls as a teen was only a reach for nurturing, and my posturing as a fly guy was merely a mask for the insecurities of a young man who did not have much.

Somehow, I always sensed those among my peers who could not stomach my natural instincts to rise above my limitations. Yet, I let them stick around anyway, believing they would witness how God works on little people just like me. His grace has never fallen short of my footsteps.

Classism is one of the biggest catalysts for jealousy and resentment from others regarding my success. I have always had less than most of my peers materially, but in substance, I have consistently proven myself to be of depth, creativity, and integrity. Because of this, I learned to guard myself against empty conversations and prying classmates who only inquired about my well-being and that of my family to keep score. I had to learn to win in their absence.

I became adept at recognizing those who wanted to stand in my light but could not take it away from me. I understood that some people thrive on the misfortunes of others, and I refused to allow their negativity to dim my shine. I focused on nurturing relationships that uplifted me, those that encouraged my growth and celebrated my achievements rather than resented them.

In this process of rebuilding, I also made it a point to reconnect with my family. I wanted to show them that I was committed to being a better person, a better father, and a better son. I reached out to those who were willing to engage with me, sharing my story and my aspirations. I wanted them to see that I was not defined by my past but by my determination to create a brighter future.

Rebuilding trust and relationships was a journey, one that required patience and effort. I knew that it would not happen overnight, but I was committed to the process. I wanted to create a new narrative for myself, one that was rooted in resilience, hope, and the belief that I could overcome the obstacles in my path. I was ready to embrace my family and friends anew, forging connections that would help me thrive in this new chapter of my life.

CHAPTER 7: SUCCESS AND IT'S DISCONTENTS

Upon my release, I hit the ground running. I had a bulletproof plan to become a barber practitioner and barbershop owner, a vision I was confident would work. I had proven to myself in prison that I could provide for my needs with my hands. The countless inmates I had laced with my razor and comb, much to their satisfaction, had given me the confidence that I was above average in the haircutting department. Cutting hair in prison was my main means of supporting myself financially, allowing me to provide for my needs when I had no money on my books to purchase necessities such as hygiene products, writing materials, and books.

Even the prison guards employed my services, and some would come to the facility off duty to be served by yours truly. This not only provided me with a steady stream of clients but also allowed me to leverage my skills to barter for things that were not available in the prison's commissary. That is when I began to see the monetary value in my barbering skills.

Within the first three months of freedom, I got OSHA certified, joined a labor union, registered for barbering at Augusta Technical College, and landed a booth in a barbershop under the apprenticeship of the shop owner. This arrangement made it legal for me to cut hair in a professional setting while I was still attending school to obtain my barber license. I was on a fast track to building the life I had always dreamed of.

With the money left over from financial aid, I purchased my first car and phone—essentials for my growth and development as a grown man, a productive citizen, and a father. These purchases symbolized my newfound independence and commitment to creating a better future for myself and my children.

However, as I began to taste success, I also encountered its discontents. The pressure to maintain my momentum was palpable. I felt the weight of expectations from both myself and those around me. Friends and family who had once doubted me now looked to me as a beacon of hope, and while I appreciated their support, it also added a layer of stress. I was determined to prove that I could succeed, but I was also acutely aware of the fragility of my circumstances.

I quickly learned that success could breed jealousy and resentment. Some of my peers, who had once celebrated my achievements, began to distance themselves. I noticed the subtle shifts in their attitudes, the way they would downplay my accomplishments or question my motives. It was disheartening, but I reminded myself that my journey was not about them; it was about me and my commitment to building a better life.

As I navigated these complexities, I also had to confront my own insecurities. The fear of failure loomed large, and I often found myself questioning whether I truly deserved the success I was achieving. I had to remind myself that I had worked hard for every step I took, that I had earned my place in this new chapter of my life.

Despite the challenges, I remained focused on my goals. I continued to hone my barbering skills, seeking out opportunities to learn and grow. I surrounded myself with positive influences, mentors who encouraged me to keep pushing forward. I understood that success was not just about achieving my goals; it was also about maintaining my integrity and staying true to myself.

In the end, I realized that success is a journey, not a destination. It comes with its own set of challenges, but it also offers the opportunity for growth and self-discovery. I was determined to embrace both the triumphs and the trials, knowing that each experience would shape me into the person I was meant to be.

CHAPTER 8: GIVING BACK AND ADVOCATING FOR CHANGE

My probation officer wanted me to host a group of probationers and parolees, hoping I could help motivate them to rise to the occasion of the course that had become my life. With all my accomplishments in such a brief period, he figured I could eliminate the excuses of former inmates who were not on my trajectory. I declined politely, telling the probation officer that I would think about it. I knew those ex-convicts needed more than just my story of readjustment to society as a catalyst for what they needed to do to get back on the right path.

Many of the people I would be talking to came from humble beginnings, just as I had. Their mental compass was often warped by the constant pressure of everyday struggles, making it difficult to focus and train their minds to push through the rubbish of life in the hood, in prison, and coming from broken homes. I understood that this was an innate quality that had to be taken into consideration when dealing with individuals who were products of their childhood environments. It would take a communal effort, an act of Congress, and a whole lot of prayer to help turn their lives around.

Instead of hosting a large group, I chose to extend my mentorship services and share my testimony with many individuals in more intimate settings. I found fulfillment in working with battered women shelters, boys' and girls' clubs, alternative schools, rescue missions, and my own students at Provision Barber College, where I worked for one of my former teachers. These environments allowed me to connect on a deeper level, offering guidance and support to those who needed it most.

In these settings, I emphasized the importance of using our stories to advocate for change. I shared my journey not just as a tale of personal triumph but as a call to action for systemic reform. I spoke about the flaws in the prison system, the lack of resources for rehabilitation, and the urgent need for a more just and rehabilitative approach. I encouraged others to join me in advocating for policies that would support education, mental health services, and job training for those who are incarcerated or recently released.

As I grew my business into a successful barbershop in a prominent area of Augusta, Georgia, I sought to give back to the community in meaningful ways. I offered my tutelage to many young barbers, and together we created an event that fostered camaraderie with the homeless, veterans, and ex-offenders who frequented the area looking for work to pay for food or shelter expenses. On the first Sunday of every month, my staff and I dedicated our time to cut hair and feed those homeless men and women that society had long neglected.

Our goal was to help them find jobs and boost their confidence by addressing their appearance. We would all eat together, share stories, and laugh, creating a sense of community and belonging. I wanted to show them that they could reclaim their lives, as I had experienced similar hardships and was still standing in the ashes of life in the same world, they felt was burning them alive.

However, after a year of these efforts, I faced challenges that forced me to readjust my focus. I learned that I had a child on the way with the woman who had accepted my hand in marriage and had been my rock since my transition back into society. My wife, Jinelys, had been by my side from the very beginning of this new journey, providing unwavering support as I navigated the complexities of entrepreneurship and community service.

With the impending arrival of our child, I realized that I needed to balance my commitments to my family and my advocacy work. While my heart remained dedicated to helping others, I understood that my family had to come first. This new chapter in my life would bring its own set of challenges, but I was determined to face them head-on, just as I had faced the shadows of my past.

Over the years, I had befriended an older gentleman named Tommy, whom most people referred to as "Unc." He was a modest fellow from Memphis, Tennessee, by way of the woods of Arkansas. A proven outdoorsman with a riddled past, Unc became a great mentor and friend, helping me stay the course as I navigated my new life. While I had received countless pats on the back and shallow comments like "Good job" or "I'm so proud of you," which were intended as words of encouragement, Unc's enthusiasm for my achievements felt among the most genuine and profound.

Somehow, I knew he had always encouraged me in the way he needed to be as a young adult navigating through life. He helped me understand that a man's value lies in what he can live without, not in his possessions. Unc led a very modest lifestyle, one in which he found joy in fishing, hunting, and gardening. He had discovered solace in being alone with the animals he raised and working on the several cars he collected or building things on his land that made him less dependent on people or systems of government.

Being around him instilled in me a greater appreciation for land development and self-sustainability. I began to see the world through a different lens, one that emphasized the importance of self-reliance and the beauty of nature. Once my barbershop grew financially, I decided to invest in a homestead on four adjoining properties, where I relocated my barbershop and began teaching my family—my wife and our three children, whom we eventually had together—how to do all the things I had observed Unc doing over the years.

We planted gardens, raised chickens, and learned the art of preserving food. I wanted my children to understand the value of challenging work and the satisfaction that comes from nurturing the land and providing for ourselves. This lifestyle not only strengthened our family bond but also reinforced the lessons I had learned from Unc about resilience and independence.

As I continued to give back to the community, I realized that my journey was not just about personal success; it was about creating a legacy for my family and those around me. I wanted to instill in my children the same values that had guided me through my struggles: the importance of community, the power of hard work, and the necessity of giving back to those in need.

Through my barbershop and the events, we organized, I aimed to create a ripple effect of positivity and support. I wanted to show others that change is possible, that they too could reclaim their lives and find purpose. My experiences with Unc and the lessons I learned from him became the foundation of my advocacy work. I understood that true success is measured not just by personal achievements but by the impact we have on others.

As I looked around at my family, my thriving business, and the community we were building, I felt a deep sense of gratitude. I was no longer just a man who had risen from the shadows; I was a father, a mentor, and a community leader. My journey was far from over, but I was committed to using my story to advocate for change and inspire others to do the same.

The simple yet practical wisdom of Uncle Tommy became the subject of many barbershop conversations. Most of my clients, family, and friends knew of him through my experiences, even though they had never been around or seen him. His lessons resonated deeply, and I often found myself sharing his insights during discussions about life, resilience, and the importance of community.

The greatest part of it all was being invested in the same community of my childhood that shaped my core values. I saw value in it, whereas most of my childhood friends had long abandoned it, no longer caring to claim ownership of the rigged existence and exposure to the crack epidemic of the '80s. The remnants of that era still lingered, casting shadows over the lives of many who remained. I felt a strong desire to support others who were incarcerated or recently released, believing that everyone deserves a second chance.

Through my experiences, I learned that while most people are trained to work for others, they should be trained to work with others and for themselves. The sense of reward that comes from employing your own talents are immeasurable. Many individuals just need someone to believe in them, to affirm that we are better than our circumstances. We are the children of the Most-High, and we must hold ourselves accountable for where we are in life as we transition into adulthood, bearing the burden of carrying our own weight.

I envisioned a more rehabilitative system—one in which individuals are not merely harvested to fulfill the occupancy of private prisons but are given the tools to grow into productive citizens. Such a system would empower those incarcerated with the skills and knowledge necessary to reintegrate into society successfully. It would provide a clean slate for those released, allowing them to apply those tools without the stigma that often accompanies a criminal record.

In my barbershop, I made it a point to create an environment that fostered growth and support. I encouraged my staff and clients to engage in conversations about change, resilience, and the importance of community. We organized workshops and events that focused on skill-building, financial literacy, and personal development. By doing so, we aimed to break the cycle of despair and hopelessness that often ensnared those who had been incarcerated.

As I continued to advocate for change, I realized that my journey was not just about my own success; it was about lifting others as I climbed. I wanted to be a beacon of hope for those who felt lost, showing them that transformation is possible. Together, we could create a community that nurtures growth, fosters understanding, and empowers individuals to reclaim their lives.

With each haircut, each conversation, and each act of kindness, I felt the weight of my purpose. I was not just a barber; I was a catalyst for change, a mentor, and a friend. My commitment to giving back and advocating for a more just and rehabilitative system was unwavering. I knew that the road ahead would be challenging, but I was ready to face it head-on, armed with the wisdom of Uncle Tommy and the belief that together, we could build a brighter future for all.

CONCLUSION: A MESSAGE OF HOPE

I wanted to use my story to advocate for prison reform because I know well, the truth in Les Brown's words: "It isn't over until you win." I worked tirelessly to convince others that they can achieve greatness if they apply the 5 P's: Proper Preparation Prevents Poor Performance. Regardless of past mistakes, they too can prevail.

My aim is to encourage readers to pursue their dreams and support one another on their journeys. My greatest passion in life has always been to become a recording artist. Although that dream took a backseat to my barbering career, I still find joy in creating music. I learned to leverage my barbering career by using music to market my services to potential clients via social media, a practice I continue to this day.

Instead of abandoning my ability to write music, poetry, or express myself creatively, I chose to elevate my skill set. I began writing movie scripts and books, often scoring them with productions that would have otherwise been reserved for songs. This led me to develop a unique genre I call "audio-movies," where stories are told cinematically through narration, poetry, and songwriting. This format allows listeners to envision the movie without seeing the film, much like a visitor at an art museum interprets what the artist is trying to convey through their work.

Sadly, some people in our society find validation in looking down on others, deriving a sense of worth from the misfortunes of those who have struggled. However, true strength lies in lifting one another up, recognizing our shared humanity, and understanding that everyone has the potential for redemption and success.

This is a call to action for readers to engage in discussions about prison reform and to support those in need. We must question the malicious intent of private prisons that depend on the criminal element to thrive to keep their doors open. The government spending allocated to building prisons could be redirected to establish trade schools and free adult training centers. Upon completion, these programs would provide job placement for participants in areas conducive to the development of the cities they live in, ensuring that tax-paying dollars benefit the communities they come from rather than lining the pockets of those invested in the prison system.

As I reflect on my journey from the shadows to success, I am filled with hope. I hope that my story inspires others to rise above their circumstances, to believe in their potential, and to support one another in the pursuit of their dreams. Together, we can create a world where everyone can thrive, regardless of their past.

NOTE TO THE READER

Dear Readers,

Thank you for taking the time to embark on this journey with me through the pages of "Breaking Chains, Building Dreams." This book is not just a reflection of my life; it is a testament to the resilience of the human spirit and the power of transformation.

As you read my story, I hope you find inspiration in the struggles and triumphs that shaped my path. My experiences have taught me that no matter how dark the shadows may seem, there is always a way to rise above them. Each of us has the potential to reclaim our lives, redefine our futures, and make a positive impact on the world around us.

I encourage you to reflect on your own journey and the journeys of those around you. Let this book serve as a reminder that we are all capable of change, growth, and success, regardless of our pasts. Together, we can foster a community of support, understanding, and hope.

Thank you for being a part of this journey. Your willingness to read and engage with these stories is a step toward creating a more compassionate and just world. Let us continue to uplift one another and advocate for change, for we are all in this together.

With gratitude and hope...

Rachaan The Barber

ORGANIZATIONS

Augusta Technical College

UGA Small Business Development Center of Augusta

Augusta Rescue Mission

Katina Burkes and Associates LLC

Boys and Girls Club of America

Provision Barber Academy

Department of Housing and Urban Development

Department of Family and Children Services

Manhood Tour (Augusta, GA)

BOOKS

Message to the Black Man by Elijah Muhammad

Go Tell It on the Mountain by James Baldwin

I Know Why the Caged Bird Sings by Maya Angelou

The 48 Laws of Power by Robert L. Greene

The New Jim Crow by Michelle Alexander

Pimp by Iceberg Slim (Robert Beck)

The Art of War by Sun Tzu

Acts of Faith by Iyanla Vanzant

Invisible Man by Ralph Ellison

Makes Me Wanna Holler by Nathan McCall

The Prisoner's Wife: A Memoir by Asha Bandele

Soledad Brothers by George Jackson

The Miseducation of the Negro by Carter G. Woodson

The Browder Files* by Anthony Browder
The Coldest Winter Ever* by Sister Souljah

ABOUT THE AUTHOR

K. Rachaan Smith, born August 14, 1976, is a passionate author and advocate from Augusta, Georgia. His journey into writing began in elementary school, where he discovered a love for storytelling that would shape his life. By high school, Rachaan had evolved into an aspiring recording artist, gaining recognition for his above-average lyrical talent.

His dreams faced an unexpected detour when he was unjustly sentenced to ten years in prison for a crime he did not commit. During this challenging chapter, Rachaan found his voice and purpose, transforming his pain into powerful narratives that resonate with many. His first book, "WHYTE PRIVILEGE: Live Audio Confessions Of Kulio Berken," showcased his unique storytelling style and established him as a writer committed to exploring the complexities of life.

In his latest work, "Breaking Chains, Building Dreams," Rachaan shares his gripping journey of resilience, redemption, and the fight for justice. This compelling memoir sheds light on the systemic barriers faced by marginalized communities, particularly young Black men, while emphasizing the importance of community support and personal growth. Through his words, Rachaan inspires others to rise above their circumstances and reclaim their dreams, proving that it is never too late to rewrite one's narrative.

www.ingramcontent.com/pod-product-compliance
Lightning Source LLC
Chambersburg PA
CBHW032102040426
42449CB00007B/1159